Heinemann

LIBRARY

A division of Reed Elsevier Inc.

V#27778

TOLL FREE ORDERS
888/454·2279
(fax) 888/844·5329

Eva Greene

SALES REPRESENTATIVE

PO BOX 2442
CALUMET CITY, IL
60409

PHONE 708-849-5257
FAX 708-849-5259

Heinemanninfo@HIL.com

The Life and Work of...

Frederic Remington

Ernestine Giesecke

Heinemann Library
Des Plaines, Illinois

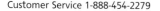

Text designed by Sandy Newell
Printed In Hong Kong/China

04 03 02 01 00
10 9 8 7 6 5 4 3 2 1

Library of Congress Cataloging-in-Publication Data
Giesecke, Ernestine, 1945-
　　　Frederic Remington / Ernestine Giesecke.
　　　　p. cm. -- (The life and work of–) (Heinemann profiles)
　　　Includes bibliographical references and index.
　　　Summary: Introduces the life and work of Frederic Remington, discussing his early years, travels in the American West, and development as an artist.
　　　ISBN 1-57572-951-2 (lib. bdg.)
　　　1. Remington, Frederic, 1861-1909 Juvenile literature.
2. Artists–United States Biography Juvenile literature.
[1. Remington, Frederic, 1861-1909. 2. Artists 3. Painting, American.　4. Art appreciation] I. Title. II. Series.
III. Series: Heinemann profiles.
N6537.R4C54　1999
709'.2—dc21
[B]
　　　　　　　　　　　　　　　　　　　　　　99-14556
　　　　　　　　　　　　　　　　　　　　　　　CIP

Acknowledgments
The Publisher would like to thank the following for permission to reproduce photographs:

Frederic Remington Art Museum, Ogdensburg, NY, pp. 4, 6, 7, 8, 9, 10, 11, 14, 18, 20, 22, 28, 29; Amon Carter Museum, Fort Worth, TX, pp. 5, 16, 21, 27; North Wind Picture Archives, Alfred, Maine, pp. 12, 26; Harpers Weekly/Magazine Memories, p. 13; Buffalo Bill Historical Center, Cody, WY, p. 15; Iris & B. Gerald Cantor Center for Visual Arts at Stanford University, Stanford Family Collections, 13932.037, p. 17; Sid Richardson Collection of Western Art, Fort Worth, TX, p. 19; ©Thomas Gilcrease Museum, Tulsa, OK, pp. 23, 25; Shidoni Foundry, p. 24.

Cover photo: *The Cowboy*, Frederic Remington/Amon Carter Museum, Fort Worth, TX

Every effort has been made to contact copyright holders of any material reproduced in this book. Any omissions will be rectified in subsequent printings if notice is given to the publisher

Some words in this book are in bold, **like this.** You can find out what they mean by looking in the Glossary.

Contents

Who Was Frederic Remington?

Frederic Remington was an American artist. He was an **illustrator**, a painter, a **sculptor**, and a writer.

Frederic Remington made pictures and **sculptures** of horses, **Indians,** and cowboys. His art tells the stories of the people who lived in the wide open spaces and **frontier towns** of the **West.**

Early Years

Frederic Remington was born October 4, 1861. He was born in Canton, New York. He was an only child. His father was a **cavalry officer** and owned a newspaper.

A Patrol.

When Frederic was 16 years old, he went to
military school. He trained to be a soldier. He
learned math and history. But he filled his
notebooks with **sketches** of horses and soldiers.

Studies at Yale

After high school, Frederic went to the Yale School of Fine Arts in Connecticut. He studied art. He played on the football team, too. Frederic is in the bottom row, on the right.

Frederic did not draw pictures of flowers and apples like the other students. Instead, he copied **casts** of old **sculptures**. This drawing by Frederic was **published** in the school newspaper.

First Trip West

When Frederic was eighteen years old, his father died. Frederic's only interests seemed to be the **West** and cowboys. He even dressed up as a cowboy for this photograph.

"And may the best man win".

Any thing for a quiet life.

When Frederic was nineteen years old, he
traveled to the West for the first time. He saw
Indians on **reservations**. He watched soldiers
taking **settlers** to and from forts. He even
bought a sheep ranch in Kansas without
seeing it first!

Making Pictures

Magazines used a special way to print the drawings Frederic made. First, the drawing was scratched onto a copper plate. Then, ink filled in the scratches on the plate. When paper was pressed onto the plate, the ink left marks on the paper.

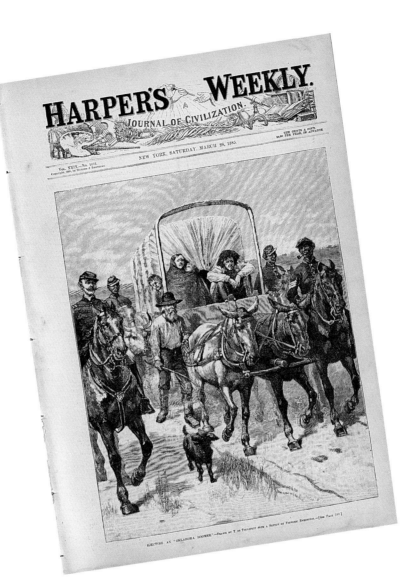

Frederic drew pen and ink drawings of the **West,** like this one. He sold the drawings to magazines in the **East**.

Drawing Real Life

In 1884, Frederic married Eva Caten. They lived in Brooklyn, New York. Magazines sent Frederic on trips to the **West**. He drew pictures of soldiers, **Indians,** cowboys, and horses.

Frederic used the **sketches** he made to remind him of what he saw. This was one way he was able to draw **accurately** how the Blackfoot people lived.

Showing Action

Frederic's drawings and paintings were full of action. The animals looked like they were leaping off the page.

16

Some people felt that Frederic did not draw animals correctly. They said that a horse would never have all four legs in the air at the same time. Then the first photographs of a horse **galloping** were made. They showed that Frederic was right!

New York Cowboy

When Frederic was 29 years old, he and his wife bought a home in New York. Frederic worked in the **studio** in his home. He continued to draw and paint.

Frederic made more trips to the **West**. He still loved the cowboy life and stories. He painted this **self-portrait** of himself as a cowboy.

Telling Stories

In the **West,** Frederic took notes about the **scenes** he **sketched.** He described exactly what he saw.

Frederic wrote short stories that explained what was happening in his paintings. He wrote books, too. The stories and books showed people in the **East** what life in the West was like.

Turning to Sculpture

Frederic wanted to make his art even more exciting. He decided to make **sculptures**. The sculptures would tell the stories of the **West**. In this photograph, Frederic is working on a clay model of a sculpture.

22

When Frederic finished the clay model, the horse looked like it was being thrown into the air. The clay model was turned into a **bronze** sculpture. Why do you think Frederic named this sculpture *The Buffalo Horse?*

Making a Bronze

Making a **bronze sculpture** requires the **skill** of many different workers. This photograph shows how bronze is poured into a mold to make a bronze sculpture.

24

Even though this sculpture is made of metal, it seems alive. You can feel the strength of the horse and the cowboy.

At the War

Frederic was interested in **military** subjects, too. In 1898, Frederic became a war **correspondent** in the Spanish-American War. Frederic is the man in the straw hat at the top left of this photograph.

Frederic joined the soldiers in Cuba as they fought in jungles and slept in the rain. He spent time with the famous Rough Riders led by **Theodore Roosevelt.**

End of the Trail

Frederic returned home to write, paint, and make **sculptures** about the **West**. In December 1909, Frederic Remington died. He was 48 years old. His **appendix** had burst. An **infection** spread through his whole body.

Frederic was known as a serious painter. He learned how to use light to show the **emotion** of the stories. This painting tells the story of the end of the cowboy, the **Indians,** and the **West** as he knew them.

Timeline

1861   Frederic Remington born, October 4

1861–65 U. S. Civil War

1876   Frederic goes to **military** school in Massachusetts
Custer's defeat at Little Big Horn

1878   Starts at Yale School of Art

1880   Frederic's father dies

1881   First trip **West**

1882   First illustration **published**

1884   Marries Eva Caten

1890   Buys home in New Rochelle, New York
Sioux defeated at Wounded Knee

1895   First book, *Pony Tracks*, published
First **sculpture,** *Bronco Buster*, completed

1898   Spanish American War
Frederic covers Spanish American War as a **correspondent**

1900   Begins making **bronze** sculptures

1909   Frederic Remington dies, December 26

Glossary

accurately correct in every way

appendix small body part near the stomach

bronze metal used to make statues

cast copy of a sculpture or statue

cavalry officer leader of a group of soldiers on horses

correspondent person who sends news to a newspaper

East part of the United States east of the Mississippi River. The area includes the states of New York, Pennsylvania, Virginia, and more.

emotion feelings about something

frontier town town at the edge of open lands

galloping moving quickly

illustrator person who draws pictures to explain a story

Indians first name given to people living in North America by explorers from Europe. They are now also called Native Americans.

infection sickness caused by germs

military having to do with armies or war

published placed in a newspaper or book for everyone to see

reservation land set aside for the use of Indians

scene place where something happens

sculptor person who makes sculptures

sculptures art made of stone or other materials

self-portrait drawing or painting of a person done by that person

settlers people who move to new places where few people lived before

sketch rough drawing

skill ability to do something well

studio place where an artist works

Roosevelt, Theodore cavalry officer and later president of the United States

West part of the United States west of the Mississippi River

Index

More Books to Read

Conlon, Laura. *Painters*. Vero Beach, Fla.: Rourke Press, Incorporated, 1994.

Pekarik, Andrew. *Sculpture*. New York: Hyperion Books for Children, 1992. An older reader can help you with this book.

Sundling, Charles W. *Cowboys of the Frontier*. Minneapolis, Minn.: ABDO Publishing Company, 1998.

Van Steenwyk, Elizabeth. *Frederic Remington*. Danbury, Conn.: Franklin Watts Inc., 1994. An older reader can help you with this book.

More Artwork to See

The Wicked Pony. 1898. Amon Carter Museum, Fort Worth, Tex.

The Smoke Signal. 1909. Amon Carter Museum, Fort Worth, Tex.

Radisson and Groseilliers. 1906. Buffalo Bill Historical Center, Cody, Wyo.

Apaches Listening. 1909. Remington Art Museum, Ogdensburg, N.Y.

The Stampede. 1909. The Gilcrease Institute of American History and Art, Tulsa, Okla.